# LOOKING FOR TARA

# LOOKING FOR TARA

## The *Gone With the Wind* Guide to
## Margaret Mitchell's Atlanta

BY DON O'BRIANT
WITH KAY O'BRIANT

LONGSTREET PRESS
Atlanta, Georgia

Published by
LONGSTREET PRESS, INC.
A subsidiary of Cox Newspapers,
A division of Cox Enterprises, Inc.
2140 Newmarket Parkway
Suite 118
Marietta, GA 30067

Printed in the United States of America
1st printing 1994

Library of Congress Catalog Card Number: 94-77585
ISBN 1-56352-172-5

Film preparation by Holland Graphics Inc., Mableton, Georgia

This book was printed by Data Reproductions, Rochester Hills, Michigan

Jacket design by Graham & Company Graphics, Inc., Atlanta, Georgia
Book design by Jill Dible

# CONTENTS

# ACKNOWLEDGMENTS

We extend our appreciation to Anne Isenhower and Franklin Garrett of the Atlanta History Center for their guidance and to Tinah Saunders for her expertise on antebellum homes in the area.

Photographs are courtesy of the *Atlanta Journal and Constitution* unless otherwise noted.

# INTRODUCTION

More than five decades after *Gone With the Wind* won the hearts of millions of fans, Margaret Mitchell's masterpiece is still a phenomenon. Each year, thousands of visitors come to Atlanta in search of the white-columned home of Scarlett O'Hara only to be told there is no Tara. It was all a product of Hollywood and Margaret Mitchell's imagination.

Actually, more Hollywood's than Mitchell's. When the designs for the movie version of Tara were being created, Mitchell kept insisting they remain true to her literary vision of Tara as a plain, columnless building in the middle of a working north Georgia plantation. The fine houses of Charleston and Natchez might have columns, but there were few in Clayton County, Georgia. As Mitchell said in a letter to Stephen Vincent Benét, "I had to ride Clayton County pretty thoroughly before I found even one white columned house in which to put the Wilkes family."

Despite Mitchell's protestations, Hollywood created an image of Tara that most of us remember and that visitors carry with them when they come to Atlanta. Finding traces of that Tara—and tangible parts of Margaret Mitchell's Atlanta—is as frustrating for tourists as the quest for the Holy Grail was for the Crusaders.

A very private person, Mitchell ordered her private papers and manuscripts burned upon her death, leaving only enough of the original manuscript to prove she wrote it. Not content to stop there with erasing her past, she left a will stipulating that her brother Stephens destroy her parents' home on Peachtree Street, possibly because she was never happy there.

Fires, neglect, and urban development finished what Margaret Mitchell and General Sherman had started. Only two of the apartments where Mitchell lived are still standing, and one—"The Dump"—is in danger of the wrecking ball.

So what's left to discover of Margaret Mitchell's real and fictional worlds? Quite a bit, if one is persistent. Many of the plantations and farmhouses that shaped the author's vision of Tara and Twelve Oaks are filled with new tenants and have been restored to look the same as they did 140 years ago. The landscape where Union and Confederate soldiers clashed has changed, but some of the terrain has not. And although restaurants have come and gone, many of the Southern dishes enjoyed in Scarlett's day are still being served in settings where the scent of magnolia blossoms and honeysuckle drift in from Southern gardens amid the sounds of cicadas and whippoorwills.

*Looking for Tara* invites visitors to retrace the footsteps of Margaret Mitchell from "The Dump," the cramped apartment where she wrote *Gone With the Wind*, to Oakland Cemetery, where she was buried after being struck by a taxi. It will escort you to Civil War battlesites and museums, into gift shops overflowing with *GWTW* memorabilia, down tree-lined roads past antebellum mansions untouched by Sherman's torch, and into restaurants where Southern hospitality is served in generous portions. So come along. You'll take a remarkable journey into a world that has been both romanticized and vilified, but one that seems destined to live on forever in the hearts of legions of fans.

# LOOKING FOR TARA

# MARGARET MITCHELL'S ATLANTA

## *Where It All Began*

**LOCATION OF MARGARET MITCHELL'S BIRTH-PLACE / 296 Cain Street near the corner of Cain and Jackson streets** ✦ Mitchell's birthplace, her grandmother Stephens's house, was a large cottage on Jackson Street that was used as a hospital during the Battle of Atlanta. In the summer of 1903, the Mitchells moved into a larger house nearby at 179 Jackson Street. All three houses were destroyed by the great fire of 1917. In her letters, Margaret Mitchell described attending a debutante party during the fire where the young debutantes worried if they would have homes to return to after the party.

Her birthplace is now a vacant lot but has a grand view of the downtown Atlanta skyline. The Jackson Street block between Cain Street and Highland Avenue is now the International Boulevard/Glen Iris exit off I-75/85 North.

**SITE OF MARGARET MITCHELL'S CHILDHOOD HOME / 179 Jackson Street ✦** The Jackson Street house, a 13-room red and yellow Victorian, was the setting for numerous childhood adventures that fueled the imagination of the future writer. As a six-year-old, she rode her roan and white pony with a group of Confederate cavalry veterans and listened raptly as they refought old battles. She also picked up a salty vocabulary that later served her well as a female journalist in a profession dominated by men.

In 1906, Mitchell got a taste of the kind of horrors Southerners faced during the Civil War. Atlanta was the scene of one of the South's worst race riots, with white gangs roaming the cities amid rumors that black mobs were planning to burn the town and cut off the water supply. The young Mitchell was alone with her father when a neighbor warned everyone to get a gun. Eugene Mitchell armed himself with a poker and an iron tool until Margaret suggested a family Confederate sword would be better. Echoes of the incident would appear years later in Mitchell's description of Scarlett and Melanie's encounter with a renegade Union soldier at Tara. And in writing about wartime in Atlanta in *Gone With the Wind*, Mitchell said she still vividly remembered the sound of gunfire from the 1906 riots as blacks, whites, and police clashed a block behind her house.

The house on Jackson Street was the scene of another childhood incident that found its way into Mitchell's fiction. As her family prepared to move to a new house on Peachtree Street, Mitchell fell and injured her leg while riding the family horse. Her injuries were far less serious than the ones Bonnie Butler suffered in *Gone With the Wind*, but they were serious enough to make Mitchell's father sell the horse and never own another. The family moved from Jackson Street to 1401 Peachtree Street in 1912.

**WASHINGTON SEMINARY SITE / Peachtree Street** ✦ This was the private prep school that Margaret Mitchell attended before entering Smith College. She was not particularly happy here, but she later praised some teachers who encouraged her writing and said they were better teachers than those at Smith. Washington Seminary was the preferred school for Atlanta's elite young women.
**Directions:** The seminary was located on Peachtree Street a few blocks north of the Mitchell house between the Equifax property and the Brookwood Amtrak Station.

**SITE OF MITCHELL HOME / 1401 Peachtree Street** ✦ A small plaque is all that remains of the house where Mitchell spent her adolescent years. White with Doric columns, the Colonial Revival two-story house was Mitchell's mother's dream house. There

*This historical marker is all that is left today to mark the location of 1401 Peachtree Street.*

was no room for stables or horses, but the wild, marshy bottomland behind the house and a privet hedge were exciting escapes where she could read or make up stories and plays. She complained that the house was always kept too cold and refused to live there after her marriage.

**JONESBORO ROAD** ✦ Georgia 54, the highway between Atlanta and Jonesboro, is crammed with service stations, convenience stores, and other urban trappings. But in Margaret Mitchell's time, it was a country road with more than its share of crumbling antebellum mansions. It was also the scene of what Mitchell called a turning point in her life. In 1907, when she was enrolled as a first grader at Forrest Avenue Elementary School, Mitchell decided she didn't want to go. As a practical lesson, Mrs. Mitchell hitched up a horse and buggy and took her recalcitrant daughter for a ride out Jonesboro Road. She pointed out the ruins of houses where wealthy people once lived, explained how the war had turned their lives upside down, and warned that education was the only security in a world of uncertainty. The message was not lost on young Margaret and appeared later in Chapter 43 of *GWTW* when Rhett Butler warns

*Maybelle Mitchell's dream house was not Margaret's favorite place. She left instructions that the house be pulled down after her death.*

*Efforts are under way to restore "The Dump," the apartment where Margaret Mitchell lived while writing* **Gone With the Wind.**

Ashley Wilkes that only those with cunning and strength will survive in a world turned upside down. It also resurfaces in the scene in Chapter 23 when Rhett abandons Scarlett and her party fleeing Atlanta on Jonesboro Road to go off and join the doomed Rebel army. By leaving her, Rhett forces Scarlett to find the determination to survive and save those dependent on her.

**THE DUMP / Crescent Avenue and Tenth Street at Peachtree Street** ✦ Margaret Mitchell called this apartment house "The Dump" when she lived here with her husband, John Marsh. Today, the term is even more fitting after years of neglect. Destined for the wrecking ball a few years ago, the house where Mitchell wrote *Gone With the Wind* is now being restored, thanks to a group of dedicated preservationists. Built in 1899 on Peachtree Street, it was moved to Crescent Avenue in 1913 to make way for commercial development. Mitchell moved into Apartment One on the bottom floor in 1925 and lived there for seven years. Preservation plans include a museum and amphitheater. A Shining Light Award gas lamp posthumously awarded her in 1965 will be re-installed in front of The Dump.

**Directions:** Take Peachtree Street north to Tenth Street. The Dump will be on your left on Crescent Avenue. Or take northbound MARTA to the Midtown Station (N4) and walk two blocks east.

**NO. 4 17TH STREET** ✦ Also known as the Russell Apartments, and just around the corner from her father's house at 1401 Peachtree Street, this was where Margaret Mitchell and John Marsh moved from The Dump in 1932. Margaret Mitchell finished *GWTW*

*No. 4 17th Street was home to the Marshes from 1932 to 1939.*

here and had begun to feel the pressures of fame after its publication in 1936. The Marshes lived in a first-floor apartment in the back of the building. The Russell Apartments were torn down in the 1980s.

THE *ATLANTA JOURNAL* AND THE *ATLANTA CONSTITUTION* BUILDING / 72 Marietta Street, N.W. (526-5286) ✦ Tucked away in a glass-enclosed compartment in the lobby is the desk that Mitchell used when she wrote for the *Atlanta Journal*'s magazine section in the 1920s. The legs of the desk and its chair were sawed off a few inches to accommodate Mitchell's diminutive frame, but there was nothing downsized about her attitude. Colleagues at the time reported that she held her own in a world biased against women reporters as she wrote articles about everyone from millionaire murderer Harry K. Thaw to Latin heartthrob and film idol Rudolph Valentino.

**Hours**: 8:00 a.m.–5:00 p.m. Monday–Friday for pre-arranged group tours only.

**Directions**: The newspaper is two blocks west of CNN Center and next door to the Federal Reserve Building on Marietta Street.

*Margaret Mitchell is shown at her desk in this publicity photo made just before* **GWTW** *was released in 1936.*

*In 1923, reporter Peggy Mitchell crawled through a window onto the roof of a hotel to interview every woman's heartthrob, Rudolph Valentino.* (Hargrett Rare Book and Manuscript Library, University of Georgia)

**GEORGIAN TERRACE / 659 Peachtree Street (897-1911)** ✦ The Georgian Terrace, formerly a grand hotel, was the scene of Mitchell's shocking Apache dance as a debutante at a charity ball on March 1, 1921. As Mitchell's partner Sigmund Weil threw her around the room in a strenuous version of the latest Paris dance rage, conservative matrons raised their cyebrows in scandalized horror. The matrons retaliated by blackballing her from the Junior League.

Later, during the 1939 premiere of *Gone With the Wind*, the stars from the movie stayed at the hotel. When the Junior League held an Old South costume ball at the City Auditorium the night before the grand premiere, Mitchell refused their invitation to be a guest of honor.

**Directions:** Drive north on Peachtree Street. The Georgian Terrace is located across the street from the Fox Theatre. Or take MARTA northbound and get off at the North Avenue station for a two-block walk.

**ATLANTA MUNICIPAL AUDITORIUM / Courtland and Gilmer streets** ✦ The facility where the Junior League Ball was held December 14, 1939, the night before the premiere, still exists. Margaret Mitchell exacted her revenge on the Junior League for blackballing her for membership almost twenty years earlier by refusing their invitation to the ball. On Courtland Street at the corner of Gilmer Street in front of Hurt Plaza, it is now the Georgia State University Alumni Hall, and houses student offices.

**FOX THEATRE / 660 Peachtree Street (876-2040)** ✦ Directly across the street from the Georgian Terrace is the Fox Theatre, a Moorish picture palace from the 1920s. Almost lost, it was saved from demolition and lovingly restored by volunteers in the 1970s. Ted Turner, who acquired the film rights to *Gone With the Wind* when he bought MGM Studios, celebrated the fiftieth anniversary of the movie here with a special "re-premiere" in 1989 of the cinematically restored film. Celebrities, special posters, and other events added to the festivities.

**Hours:** Tours are available year round at 10:00 a.m. on Mondays and Thursdays, 10:00 a.m. and 11:30 a.m. on Saturdays.

**Admission:** $5 for adults, $4 senior citizens, $3 students.

**Directions:** Drive north on Peachtree or take MARTA and get off at the North Avenue Station (N3) a couple of blocks east.

**ONE SOUTH PRADO** ✦ Mitchell and her husband John Marsh lived in Apartment 4 of what was then

*The crowd welcomes celebrities as well as original cast members at the Fox Theatre celebration of the fiftieth anniversary of the premiere of GWTW.*

*Margaret Mitchell and her husband lived above the double door-way at One South Prado from 1939 until her death.*

*Margaret Mitchell shows off a few of the foreign editions of* GWTW *in her apartment on The Prado.*

called Della Manta Apartments from 1939 to 1949. As a plaque on the building notes, most of the manuscript of *Gone With the Wind* was burned in the boiler room by Mitchell's secretary and the building custodian the day after her death. (Mitchell left instructions that this be done.) The building is now a condominium complex occupied by other tenants.

**Directions**: From downtown Atlanta, go north on Piedmont Avenue for 15 blocks. The Prado is on the left across from Piedmont Park.

**ACCIDENT SCENE / Peachtree and Thirteenth streets** ✦ On August 11, 1949, Mitchell and her husband were preparing to cross Peachtree Street at the Atlanta Women's Club to see *The Canterbury Tales* film showing at the Arts Theatre. A speeding taxi rounded the blind curve, and she panicked and darted into the path of the vehicle. Mitchell died from brain damage at noon on August 16. The driver of the taxi died in Georgia in April 1994.

**OAKLAND CEMETERY / 240 Oakland Avenue, S.E. (688-2107)** ✦ When Margaret Mitchell was buried in Oakland Cemetery on a hot, humid August 17, 1949, only 300 invited guests were allowed to attend. After the service, the public swarmed in and

took funeral flowers as souvenirs. Mitchell joined
famous Atlantans from governors to generals who
had been laid to rest here since 1850. The cemetery
was a favorite spot for nineteenth-century
Atlantans, who often spent Sunday afternoons tend-
ing family plots and picnicking under the tall oaks.
The southeast Atlanta park, with its statuary and
marble mausoleums adorned with stained glass, still
offers an opportunity to dip into local history and
Victorian art while strolling under some of Atlanta's
oldest magnolia trees. A marker shows the location
where General John B. Hood, commander of the
Confederate troops during the Battle of Atlanta,
watched the fighting from a second-story balcony of
a house that stood on property now in the cemetery.

*The hearse bearing Mitchell's casket leaves Spring Hill, a Patterson
Funeral Home, August 17, 1949. The funeral was limited to 300
close friends by invitation only.*

*Margaret Mitchell Marsh was buried beside her husband and behind her father and mother in Oakland Cemetery.*

**Hours:** The cemetery is open daily, 8:00 a.m.–6:00 p.m. The office is open Monday–Friday, 9:00 a.m.–5:00 p.m., with group tours available by appointment for 10 or more people.

**Admission:** Free. A brochure with a map of famous graves in the cemetery is available for $1.25.

**Directions:** Exit on the Martin Luther King Jr. Drive exit off I-85/75 and go east. The street dead-ends at the cemetery gate.

## MARGARET MITCHELL SQUARE / Intersection of Peachtree and Forsyth streets and Carnegie Way

✦ This downtown Atlanta area has several ties to

Margaret Mitchell. The pink granite Georgia-Pacific headquarters on Peachtree Street is built on the site of the Loew's Grand Theatre where *Gone With the Wind* had its premiere on December 15, 1939. The movie was re-premiered here in 1947, 1954, 1961, and 1967. The theater burned in 1979. There is an inscription in the wall to the right of the main entrance to the Georgia-Pacific building (look for the misspelling).

The Atlanta/Fulton County Public Library at 1 Margaret Mitchell Square is built on the site of an earlier building, the Carnegie Library. Margaret Mitchell used the Carnegie Library for research when writing *Gone With the Wind*, and, according to reports, the petite author used to dig through bound copies of Civil War–era newspapers in the basement by lying on the floor with the heavy volumes propped open on her stomach so she could maneuver them. An exhibit of Mitchell's original typewriter, manuscript pages, family photographs, signed copies of *Gone With the Wind*, and lobby cards from the movie is set up inside the library.

Across from the Georgia-Pacific building and the library is a recent memorial to Margaret Mitchell, a public space with a fountain, an inscription, and a modern statuary designated as Margaret Mitchell Memorial Square.

**Library hours:** 9:00 a.m.–6:00 p.m. Monday; 9:00 a.m.–8:00 p.m. Tuesday–Thursday; 9:00 a.m.–5:00 p.m. Friday; 10:00 a.m.–5:00 p.m. Saturday; 2:00 p.m.–6:00 p.m. Sunday.

**Directions:** The library is where Forsyth Street,

Carnegie Way, and Peachtree Street converge, one block east of Woodruff Park at Atlanta's famous Five Points.

*Loew's Grand Theatre is aglow the night of GWTW's 1939 premiere.*

**THE ROAD TO TARA MUSEUM / 659 Peachtree Street (897-1939)** ✦ It is fitting that this museum and gift shop is located in the Georgian Terrace, for this former hotel is where Margaret Mitchell reluctantly handed over the *GWTW* manuscript to Macmillan editor Harold Latham. Located in the lower level of the renovated Georgian Terrace, the Road to Tara Museum offers a range of exhibits on Margaret Mitchell, her book, and the movie. Browse among the displays of photos, newspapers, and other artifacts dealing with Atlanta during the Civil War years, or view a documentary film about Mitchell and the Margaret Mitchell House, Inc., the group raising funds to restore The Dump. Exhibits include a collection of one hundred different commemorative *GWTW* dolls, displays from the filming of *GWTW*, reproduced costumes, a collection of international editions, and autographed copies of *GWTW* and other books by Southern writers. The gift shop offers prints by Southern artists and *GWTW* souvenirs.

**Hours**: The museum is open Monday–Saturday, 10:00 a.m.–6:00 p.m., and Sunday, 1:00 p.m.–6:00 p.m.

**Admission**: $5 adults, $4.25 seniors, $3.50 students. Children under 11 free.

**Directions**: Drive north on Peachtree Street. The Georgian Terrace is located across the street from the Fox Theatre. Or take MARTA northbound and get off at the North Avenue station for a two-block walk.

*Debbie Kines shows off her collection of* Gone With the Wind *dolls at the Road to Tara Museum.*

**HERITAGE ROW / 55 Upper Alabama Street (584-7879)** ✦ For visitors pressed for time, Heritage Row museum at Underground Atlanta offers a quick, hands-on look at Atlanta's past. Note the large glass etching of Margaret Mitchell and Scarlett O'Hara on the windows alongside likenesses of Martin Luther King, Jr.; Confederate General Joseph Johnson; newspaper editor Henry Grady; baseball home-run king Hank Aaron; and Coca-Cola executive Robert W. Woodruff. Step inside, and you're immediately in the midst of the sights and sounds of history. Touch a real bale of cotton and listen to a railroad whistle blow. Walk into a crudely constructed Civil War bomb shelter and hear the sounds of bombing mingled with the voices of historical figures. Examine photographs of Atlanta during and after the Civil War and see the price the city paid under General Sherman's campaign.

As you walk closer to the present, videos, audio messages from historical figures, sounds of construction, and blues music re-create significant events of the nineteenth and twentieth centuries.

When you're finished, stop in the adjoining gift shop and browse among *GWTW* posters, postcards, games, curios, and other mementos of Atlanta's history.

**Hours:** 10:00 a.m.–5:00 p.m. Tuesday–Saturday; 1:00 p.m.–5:00 p.m. Sunday.

**Admission:** $4 adults; $3 senior citizens and members of tour groups; $2 children 3–12. Children under 2 free.

**Directions:** Museum is located at 55 Upper Alabama Street between Pryor Street and Central Avenue. If taking MARTA, get off at the Five Points Station and exit to Peachtree Street across from Underground Atlanta.

**OMNI *GWTW* MUSEUM / 100 Techwood Avenue, S.W.** ✦ Scheduled to open in January 1995, this museum at the CNN Center will display a large collection of *GWTW* memorabilia from the collection of Herb Bridges. Plans include round-the-clock showings of *GWTW* on TV monitors. Museum-quality items will be offered for sale. The museum adds a *GWTW* dimension to the Omni's other offerings, the CNN Tour, the Turner Store, and the varied shops and restaurants in the mall.

**The Turner Store**, also located in CNN Center, sells *GWTW* souvenirs, including the *GWTW* game, chocolates, posters, T-shirts, commemorative plates and playing cards.

**Directions**: The CNN Center is located in downtown Atlanta in the same complex as the Omni Hotel and Omni sports arena. If taking MARTA, exit at the Omni station on the West Line.

**HERB BRIDGES** ✦The author of several books on *GWTW*, Herb Bridges has the world's largest collection of *GWTW* items. Bridges also is available for lectures and special group presentations. He can be reached at 404-253-4934 or at P.O. Box 192, Sharpsburg, GA 30277.

**MICHAEL MOTES** ✦ A long-time *GWTW* fan, Michael Motes organized the Crescent Avenue Yacht Club, an informal group interested in Margaret Mitchell and her book. He also has a collection and presents programs for groups. His collection includes unpublished photographs of Margaret

*Herb Bridges with a display of the Spanish movie poster of* GWTW.

Mitchell, memorabilia, foreign editions of *GWTW* in 27 languages, and other items. He can be reached at 429-8262.

**ATLANTA CELEBRITY WALK / 235 International Boulevard** ✦ One block east of the Omni is the Atlanta Celebrity Walk on the sidewalk in front of the Atlanta Chamber of Commerce between Walton and Marietta streets. Markers of granite and bronze honor Margaret Mitchell and thirteen other famous Georgians.

**MARGARET MITCHELL FAYETTE COUNTY LIBRARY / 155 South Jeff Davis Drive, Fayetteville (404-461-8841)** ✦ In the 1940s, Margaret Mitchell heard about a group of Fayette County women who were raising money to build a public library by selling aprons, jams, and jellies. She donated copies of *GWTW* along with other books to build a book collection and every year sent a donation to help their cause. She visited the newly opened facility in 1949 and gave permission for the library to be officially called the Margaret Mitchell Fayette County Library in honor of her relatives who came from the vicinity. After her death later that year, the library received one of only two Mitchell bequests through

her will. (The other went to the Atlanta Historical Society, which was co-founded by her father.) The library features a Margaret Mitchell display in the reading room of *GWTW* foreign editions, dolls, collectibles, newspaper articles, and memorabilia.
**Hours:** 9:00 a.m.–9:00 p.m. Monday–Thursday; 9:00 a.m.–6:00 p.m. Friday and Saturday; closed Sundays.
**Directions:** Take I-285 to I-75 south and get off at the first exit to Riverdale on Highway 85. Go through Riverdale to Fayetteville and turn left at the second traffic light onto Jeff Davis Drive. Go two miles and look for signs two blocks on the right after crossing Highway 54.

**THE FAYETTE COUNTY HISTORICAL SOCIETY / Lee Street and Johnson Way, Fayetteville (404-461-2000)** ✦ Housed in the original 1947 Fayette Library building, the historical society has a collection of some Margaret Mitchell materials and is working to establish a definitive research center on Mitchell and *GWTW* in the areas of local history and Mitchell family genealogy.
**Hours:** 6:00 p.m.–9:00 p.m. Tuesdays; 10:00 a.m.–1:00 p.m. Thursdays; 9:00 a.m.–1:00 p.m. Saturdays.
**Directions:** Take I-285 to I-75 south and get off at the first exit to Riverdale on Highway 85. Go through Riverdale to Fayetteville and turn left at the second traffic light onto Jeff Davis Drive. Johnson Way is the second right off Jeff Davis from the Highway 54/Jeff

Davis Intersection. The historical society building is across the street from the fire station.

# Library Collections

**ROBERT W. WOODRUFF LIBRARY / Emory University (727-6887)** ✦ The Margaret Mitchell Collection is housed on the top floor of the Woodruff Library. It consists of nine boxes of correspondence, four containers of oversized items such as posters, and foreign language translations of *GWTW* and various *GWTW* editions. The librarians are very friendly and say visitors are welcome.

**Directions**: Take I-285 East to U.S. 78; go toward Decatur. U.S. 78 turns into Scott Blvd. at Market Square Mall. Go right at the third stop light on North Decatur Road and go two miles to Clifton Road. Turn right into Emory. Take second left at Asbury Terrace. The Woodruff Library is the tall tower in front of you.

**Hours**: Monday–Friday, 8:30 a.m.–5:30 p.m., Saturday, 9:00 a.m.–5:30 p.m.

**HARGRETT RARE BOOK AND MANUSCRIPT LIBRARY / University of Georgia, Athens (706-542-7123)** ✦ For scholarly perusal of Margaret Mitchell's letters, papers, and photographs, this is the place to go. The collection is open to the public, although the library prohibits photocopies of the materials.

**Hours:** 8:00 a.m.–5:00 p.m. Monday–Friday; 9:00 a.m.–5:00 p.m. Saturday. Closed Sunday.

**Directions:** Athens is about 65 miles east of Atlanta on U.S. 29, U.S. 78, or Highway 316. As you enter downtown Athens on Broad Street, turn right onto Jackson Street, the first street past the arches at the front of the historic University of Georgia campus. The library is the tallest building on the right.

*See also listings for Atlanta History Center and Atlanta/Fulton County Library.*

**BARNSLEY GARDENS / Cartersville (706-773-7480)** ✦ Barnsley Gardens is a historic plantation with a ruined plantation house about 60 miles north of Atlanta. It was used as the setting for *St. Elmo*, an 1866 popular romantic novel by Augusta Jane Evans Wilson that some say contributed to Margaret Mitchell's view of the South. The family's history is indeed stranger than fiction. Godfrey Barnsley came to Savannah from England in the 1820s, made his fortune as a cotton broker, and married Julia Scarborough, a wealthy merchant's daughter. He built a house, Woodlands, on 10,000 acres in Bartow County and began developing the gardens, but because he was an Englishman, he did not believe in slavery. Instead, he hired pensioners and sharecroppers to work his cotton acreage. After Julia died in the

*Barnsley Gardens historian Clent Coker stands before the ruins of Woodlands.*

1850s, Barnsley was often seen walking in the gardens speaking to his wife's ghost and asking advice on the house or the gardens. Two of his sons and a son-in-law fought in the Civil War. A daughter, Julia, married a German whose father was a successful blockade runner during the Civil War. After the war the sons, George and Lucien Barnsley, both refused to take the loyalty oath and emigrated to Brazil. The family lost its fortune and later moved into a separate kitchen house after a tornado blew the roof off Woodlands in 1906. Mitchell knew of the Barnsleys and apparently used some parts of their story in *GWTW*. The successful blockade runner, Civil War looting, poverty and hardship after the war, and other elements such as the dark hero typified in *St. Elmo* show up in her book.

**Directions:** Take I-75 north from Atlanta approximately 60 miles to exit 128. Turn left at the exit and go 1.5 miles on Highway 140; turn left at Hall Station Road and go 5.5 miles to the Barnsley Gardens sign. Turn right on Barnsley Gardens Road; go 2.5 miles. Barnsley Gardens is on the left.

**Hours:** 10:00 a.m.–6:00 p.m. Tuesday–Saturday; 12:00 p.m.–6:00 p.m. Sunday.

**THE ATLANTA HISTORY CENTER / 3101 Andrews Drive, N.W. (814-4000)** ✦ There's always an exhibit of some sort about *GWTW*, Margaret Mitchell, or the Civil War at the history center. "Disputed Territories:

*The Tullie Smith House at the Atlanta History Center is what a real north Georgia antebellum plantation house looked like.*

*Gone With the Wind* and Southern Myths" is on display until the end of 1994. "Gone for a Soldier: Transformed by War, 1861–1865" is showing through December 1995. Both exhibits reveal what life was really like, and it wasn't all hoop skirts and mint juleps. The *GWTW* exhibit features descriptions from the book and images from the movie along with letters, diaries, photographs, and period clothing, including a corset and Scarlett O'Hara's black mourning hat and veil. Other parts of the exhibit examine women's roles in the mid-1800s and question the accuracy of the descriptions of slavery in *GWTW*.

For a realistic look at a pre–Civil War farm, walk over to the Tullie Smith Farm on the grounds of the Atlanta History Center. This is an example of a working farm with a plantation-plain house, barn, smokehouse, corn crib, blacksmith shop, and log cabin. Sometimes tours include demonstrations of nineteenth-century crafts, and each spring the Sheep to Shawl Day features sheepshearing, spinning, and weaving demonstrations.

In the Museum of Atlanta History, walk through 165 years of Atlanta history in the "Metropolitan Frontiers" exhibit and see the various stages of Atlanta's development from the days of Indian settlements through the Civil War, *Gone With the Wind*, the civil rights movement, and the Olympic Games campaign. Hundreds of historic photographs, artifacts, video presentations, and special areas for hands-on exploration make history come alive. And right in the middle of the exhibit are an 1890s shotgun house moved from southwest Atlanta and an 1898 horse-drawn fire engine used in Atlanta's tragic fire of 1917—a conflagration that left a lasting impression on a young Margaret Mitchell and undoubtedly kindled her imagination when she was writing about General Sherman's visit in her novel.

Next door to the Atlanta history museum is McElreath Hall, with a library of one of the largest Margaret Mitchell collections open to the public.

More *GWTW* and Mitchell memorabilia are for sale in the gift shop in the history museum. A brochure about the museum's fiftieth anniversary exhibit, "*GWTW*: The Facts about the Fiction," is available. The gift shop also offers a good selection of books on Margaret Mitchell, *GWTW*, and the Civil War, as well as posters, mugs, T-shirts, postcards and other gift items with a *GWTW* theme.

**Hours**: Atlanta History Center: 9:00 a.m.–5:30 p.m. Monday–Saturday; noon–5:30 p.m. Sunday.
Gift shop: 10:00 a.m.–5:00 p.m. Monday–Saturday; noon–5:00 p.m. Sunday.
**Admission**: $6 for adults; $4.50 students and senior citizens; $3 for youths 6–17; children under 5 free. Free on Thursdays after 1:00 p.m. Group rates available.
**Directions**: Take I-75 to the West Paces Ferry exit and go east for about two miles. Turn right on Andrews Drive and take the first driveway on the left. On MARTA, get off at the Lenox Station and get on bus no. 23 to Peachtree Street and West Paces Ferry Road. Andrews Drive is three blocks west.

**ATLANTA MUSEUM / 537 Peachtree Street (872-8233)** ✦ This museum in a 1900-era private house has Eli Whitney's first cotton gin (circa 1794), a Japanese Zero from World War II, and a significant collection of Margaret Mitchell memorabilia. More than 350 books from Mitchell's personal library are here, but, unfortunately, Mitchell's secretary was ordered to tear out the autographed flyleaf pages before they were sold to the museum. The rest of Mitchell's belongings are an eclectic collection of wastebaskets, a gas stove, her World War II air-raid helmet, linens and glassware from her apartment, and, most puzzling of all since Mitchell and her husband lived in apartments, a push lawnmower.

Mitchell purchased Civil War letters from museum owner Jim Elliott's father in the 1920s for research on what later turned out to be *GWTW*. Mitchell was a family friend, and Elliott remembers that she dropped by the museum only two weeks before her death.

According to Elliott, when the Mitchell family's house on Peachtree was being taken down after Margaret Mitchell's death (upon her instructions), a cousin of Elliott bought the columns, some windows, the front door, and other portions of the exterior for use in an unidentified house in Swainsboro.

**Hours:** Open by appointment for group tours (872-8233).

**Directions:** Go north on Peachtree Street from downtown. The museum is in a house across the street from Crawford Long Hospital.

**THE CYCLORAMA / 800 Cherokee Avenue, S.E. (624-1071 or 658-7625)** ✦ Other than participating in a reenactment, this exhibit is about as close as any of us will get to the Civil War. The Cyclorama at Grant Park houses a circular painting 42 feet tall and more than 350 feet long of the Battle of Atlanta. Painted in 1884, it was bought at an auction in 1890 and housed in a fireproof circular building in Grant Park in 1921. During the 1930s, figures, mannequins, and models were added to a diorama in front of the painting. Restored in the early

*Vivien Leigh and Clark Gable walk the Cyclorama during festivities leading to the movie premiere on December 15, 1939.*

1980s, it has remained one of Grant Park's most popular attractions.

A revolving platform inside the theater slowly moves visitors around the painting while a recorded narration explains the action scenes. (Look for the figure of Rhett Butler that was added to the diorama in the 1940s, due to repeated requests by tourists.) The Cyclorama also has an exhibit and artifacts on the Atlanta Campaign and the Texas, one of the locomotives involved in the Great Locomotive Chase that began in Kennesaw in 1862.

At the southeast corner of Grant Park (Boulevard

and Atlanta Avenue) is a historical marker for Fort Walker and some of the last remaining fortifications from the Battle of Atlanta.

**Hours:** 9:20 a.m.–4:30 p.m. daily, October–May; 9:20 a.m.–5:30 p.m. daily, June–September.

**Admission:** $3.50 adults; $3 senior citizens; $2 children 6–12; children under 6 free. Call 658-7625 for group rates.

**Directions:** Take I-20 to the Boulevard exit. Signs will direct you to Grant Park and the Cyclorama. At the southeast corner of Grant Park are Fort Walker and the last remaining fortifications from the Battle of Atlanta.

**STONE MOUNTAIN PARK / U.S. Highway 78, Stone Mountain (498-5690 or 498-5600) ✦** The world's largest granite outcropping has another claim to fame: carved in the side of the mountain are much larger-than-life likenesses of Confederate generals Robert E. Lee and Stonewall Jackson and Confederate president Jefferson Davis. The park has many recreational attractions, including a waterslide, riverboat rides, boat rentals, railroad rides, and miniature golf, but those interested in the period of *GWTW* should visit the antebellum plantation complex. Nineteen authentic buildings were moved from their original sites throughout Georgia to re-create a representative Georgia plantation of the 1840s. Buildings range from a 1780s cottage to a big house from pre–Civil War days. The Antebellum Festival in the

*The Stone Mountain Plantation House reflects a bygone era.*

spring and the Yellow Daisy Festival in the fall offer living exhibits, cooking, and crafts demonstrations.

At the base of the carving, Memorial Hall houses a museum of Civil War uniforms, weaponry, and artifacts. Don't miss the evening laser show during the summer months when thousands spread picnic suppers on the grassy meadow between Memorial Hall and the carving and watch high-tech fireworks accompanied by music. One of the most popular numbers is the climax during Elvis Presley's rendition of the trilogy "All My Troubles," "Battle Hymn of the Republic," and "Dixie." The carving seems to come to life and the figures gallop off the mountain.

Still want to see more stuff about the Civil War? Then visit Confederate Hall near the West Gate for "The War in Georgia," a multimedia exhibit of photos and troop movements on a lighted map. Narration

*The carving on Stone Mountain looks down over the park's many attractions.*

and displays explain the battles of the Atlanta Campaign and Sherman's March to the Sea.

**Hours:** The park is open 6:00 a.m.–midnight daily year round. The plantation area is open 10:00 a.m.–8:00 p.m. in the summer; 10:00 a.m.–5:00 p.m. September–May. Closed December, January, and February.

**Admission:** $5 per car to get into the park. The War in Georgia exhibit and the Civil War Museum are free. $3 per person for the Antebellum Plantation complex.

**Directions:** Take I-285 to U.S. 78/Stone Mountain Freeway. The park entrance is a couple of miles east on Stone Mountain Freeway on your right.

# THE SCARLETT EXPERIENCE

## *Tours and Events with an Old South Flavor*

**LOVEJOY PLANTATION / Jonesboro (478-6807)** ✦ For groups of thirty-five or more, owner Betty Talmadge offers a multi-sensory taste of the Old South with tours of Lovejoy, her antebellum plantation, reenactments of Confederate cavalry raids, and Southern feasts that guarantee you'll never be hungry again (at least for several hours). Visitors also can see the Fitzgerald farmhouse (home of Margaret Mitchell's great-grandparents and a possible model for Tara) that Talmadge bought and moved to the grounds. Talmadge claims the Lovejoy mansion was an inspiration for Ashley Wilkes's Twelve Oaks, but you'll have to judge for yourself.

Mrs. Talmadge does, indeed, provide a complete Southern experience. At the parties she trots out tame wildlife such as Rabbit E. Lee, Billy T. Sherman the goat, Ulysses S. Grunt the pig, and Assley T. Wilkes

*Betty Talmadge's Lovejoy Plantation. The Fitzgerald farmhouse is also on the grounds.*

the donkey and shows flatlanders an old moonshine still that is set up for demonstration purposes. Later, visitors can dine on fried chicken, Talmadge Farms country ham, Rhett Butter Biscuits, Confederate Cucumber Mousse, grits casserole, pecan tassies, and Confederate Minié Balls (sausage cheese biscuits) or barbecue and Brunswick stew while some of Mrs. Talmadge's rowdy friends dress in Confederate gray, mount their horses, draw their sabers, and conduct a cavalry raid complete with blood-curdling rebel yells.

**Directions**: Lovejoy Plantation is located about 30 miles south of Atlanta in Henry County on U.S. 19 and 41. Betty Talmadge cannot accommodate surprise visitors, so call ahead for reservations (404-478-6807).

**INN SCARLETT'S FOOTSTEPS / 138 Hill Street, Concord (800-886-7355)** ✦ If you can't spend the night at Tara or Twelve Oaks, this is the next best thing. K. C. Bassham's plantation mansion 45 minutes south of Hartsfield International Airport is a bed-and-breakfast decked out with scads of *GWTW* memorabilia. Guests can stay in rooms named for *GWTW* characters—Scarlett, Rhett, Gerald O'Hara, Ashley, and Melanie. Each room has a private bath. Since news of Inn Scarlett's Footsteps began spreading after its opening in October 1993, a steady stream of tour groups, retirees, church groups, and international tourists have found their way to Concord to stay overnight or to visit the gift shop and museum rooms or eat at the long dining room table.

Ms. Bassham has added catered lunches to her breakfast menu and has produced a video on the experience with her daughter as a Scarlett lookalike. She also will put on costume balls and provide the costumes. And *GWTW* fans apparently never take holidays. "I was even full on Christmas Eve," she says.

**Prices**: Rooms rent from $65 nightly. Tours are available at $5 for adults, $4 for senior citizens, and $3 for

*K. C. Bassham, owner of Inn Scarlett's Footsteps, stands in the midst of her* GWTW *collection at her bed and breakfast in Concord, Georgia.*

children. Ask about special package tours with a catered lunch.

**Directions:** Take I-75 south to exit 77 and follow the

signs to Griffin. From Griffin, take Highway 19 to Zebulon. Go right at the traffic light in Zebulon to Highway 18 to Concord. The inn is 4/10 mile from Strickland's Store on the right.

*Inn Scarlett's Footsteps welcomes all seeking a true* GWTW *experience.*

**MANSIONS AND MAGNOLIAS / Newnan (252-2109)** ✦
Carolyn Ashworth offers the next best thing to a trip
to Tara. Her private tours of the antebellum homes in
Newnan (about 45 minutes south of Atlanta) provide a
close-up view of life before the Civil War. Many of the
old houses in Newnan were spared by Sherman
because the town was a hospital center for both sides.

On request, Ms. Ashworth will organize a plantation dress-up dinner party with banjos and barbecue.
She customizes her tours for each group, tailoring
content and length for specific requests.

**Directions**: Sites vary, so directions will be given
when you call to set up the tour.

# BEYOND TARA

## *Where Scarlett's Neighbors Lived*

Most early residents of Georgia did not live in white-columned mansions, of course. And those who did started out in much humbler dwellings, usually simple "dog-trot" houses with an open-air hallway between two rooms. As more land was cleared and cotton prices rose, so did the roofs. More rooms were added and a stairway built. Prosperous planters eventually added wings, facades, and the gleaming white columns that Hollywood latched onto in *Gone With the Wind* and other movies as symbols of the Old South.

General Sherman did his part to destroy these mansions—and thus the spirit of the South—and time, fires, and neglect did the rest. But some still exist in Atlanta and are as close as a 30-minute drive from downtown. They're not Tara, but they are representative of the kind of homes Scarlett's neighbors would have lived in. Just a glimpse of the white exteriors set against a green backdrop of magnolia trees is enough to stir the imagination of the visitor—just as it certainly stirred the imagination of Margaret Mitchell.

# Roswell Historic Homes

Just 20 miles north of Atlanta off Georgia 400 is the city of Roswell, founded by Roswell King in 1839. It began as a manufacturing town, using the Chatta-hoochee River to power a textile mill. Roswell's homes were designed by an architect from Connecti-cut who built elegant country homes for family mem-bers and investors in the mill. The cool summers also attracted low-country planters fleeing yellow fever. Although Union troops captured the town during the Civil War, destroyed the mill, and deported the women workers, the homes and the town were spared. Visitors can walk through the halls of these elegant homes, dine in historic buildings, poke among the ruins of the mill on the river, and browse through shops on the square. For a complete tour of the Roswell area, contact the Roswell Historical Soci-ety, 935 Alpharetta Street (992-1665), or stop at the Roswell Visitors Center, 617 Atlanta Street (640-3253). Here are some highlights of the tour:

**BULLOCH HALL / 180 Bulloch Avenue (992-1731)** ✦
One of the most impressive Roswell houses is Bulloch Hall, built in 1840 by Maj. James Stephens Bulloch, the grandfather of President Theodore Roosevelt. The

president's parents, Mittie Bulloch and Theodore Roosevelt, Sr., were married in the dining room of the Greek Revival mansion in 1853.

**Hours:** 11:00 a.m.–2:00 p.m. Thursdays and Fridays; 2:00 p.m.–4:00 p.m. Sundays.

**Admission:** $3.

**Directions:** Take I-285 to the Roswell Road exit and go north to the town square in Roswell. Turn left onto Georgia 120, right on Mimosa, and left on Bulloch Avenue.

*Bulloch Hall is owned by the city of Roswell and is often host to festivals and activities.*

**PRIMROSE COTTAGE / 674 Mimosa Boulevard, Roswell (594-2299)** ✦ This cottage was the first house built in Roswell in 1839 for Roswell King, his widowed daughter, Eliza Hand, and her children. The wooden fence that spans the yard is original and has hand-carved spindles made of rosemary pine.
**Hours**: 11:00 a.m.–3:00 p.m. Wednesdays; 10:00 a.m.–2:00 p.m. Saturdays. Guided tours at 1:00 p.m. and 2:00 p.m. both days.
**Admission**: $3. Group rates available.
**Directions**: Take I-285 to the Roswell Road exit and go north on Highway 9 to the town square in Roswell. Turn left onto Georgia 120, right on Mimosa. Or take Highway 400 north 12.5 miles above I-285 to the Northridge Exit, go left to Highway 9/Atlanta Street, then drive 7 miles to the center of Roswell.

# Newnan Historic Homes

The town of Newnan, located about 40 miles southwest of Atlanta, was founded in 1828 by a group of Baptists. With the coming of the railroads, the town grew prosperous and large homes were built by wealthy cotton planters. The elegant antebellum homes here were spared during the Civil War because the town served as a hospital center that treated both Union and Confederate troops in seven hospitals.

*The Don Dietz House in Newnan is an example of the antebellum mansions left untouched by war.*

NEWNAN-COWETA HISTORICAL SOCIETY / **Temple Avenue and College Street (404-252-2270)** ✦ Except for fall and spring tours, Newnan's historic homes are not open to the public. But for a brochure of the town's self-guided driving tour featuring 22 historic homes, stop by the historical society. Here are some of the tour's highlights: **Rosemary / LaGrange Street** ✦This simple frame house is typical of the kind of homes constructed by the first settlers in the county. Built in 1828 by Dr. Joel Wingfield Terrell, it was moved from its original location. **Dent-Walls Home /52 College Street** ✦ This house, built in 1854 by Joseph Ephraim Dent, has four fluted Doric columns, a center hall, and four exterior chimneys. The doors and windows with sidelights are a trademark of Coweta County homes. **Sargent-Estanich Home / 47 Jackson Street** ✦ This 1840 Greek Revival house is one of the few that remain in their original form. The center hall has the original walls of hand-dressed tongue-and-groove pine boards in contrast with the plastered formal rooms.

**Hours**: The Newnan-Coweta Historical Society is open 10:00 a.m.–noon and 1:00 p.m.–3:00 p.m. Tuesdays, Wednesdays, and Thursdays; 2:00 p.m.–5:00 p.m. Saturdays and Sundays.

**Directions**: Take I-85 south to the Newnan exit and follow signs to downtown.

# Marietta Historic Homes

Marietta, located 25 miles northwest of Atlanta on I-75, was founded in 1834 as a farming community. When the railroad arrived, it brought in wealthy families seeking relief from the heat and disease of coastal summers. A thriving resort industry grew up around many of the natural springs. Hotels were built, including the Kennesaw House, now the home of the Trackside Grille Restaurant. This is the hotel where wartime spies plied their trade and General Sherman slept before marching to Atlanta. As he left town, however, he burned only the courthouse and surrounding businesses and spared most of the homes.

MARIETTA WELCOME CENTER / 429-1115 ✦ The
Welcome Center is located in the old depot west of
the Marietta square along the railroad tracks. Visitors
can take-a walking or driving tour of 52 Marietta
homes and public buildings, but, except for special
tours at Christmas and in the spring, none of the
houses are open to the public. Free brochures featuring pictures of the houses, a map, and history of the
houses are available at the Welcome Center.

Some highlights of the tour: **Tranquilla / Kennesaw Avenue** ✦ Located about a mile from the square,
this impressive white-columned house survived
because its mistress refused to leave her beloved home
when it was commandeered by Union officers during
the war. **Oakton / Kennesaw Avenue** ✦ Originally a
white-columned house in 1838, Oakton was updated
after the war to a mid-Victorian style. John N.
Wilder of Savannah bought the house in 1852 as a
summer residence. The house was headquarters to
Union general W. W. Loring during the Battle of
Kennesaw Mountain.

**Hours:** The Marietta Welcome Center is open 10:00
a.m.–3:00 p.m. Monday–Saturday, 1:00 p.m.–4:00
p.m. Sunday.

**Admission:** For $4, you can rent a tape and cassette
recorder with information about the homes on a self-
guided tour.

**Directions:** Take I-75 north from Atlanta and drive
17 miles. Take exit 112 (South Marietta Loop) and
go 3.5 miles to the Welcome Center in the downtown historic district between Whitlock Avenue and
Green Street.

# Madison Historic Homes

Founded in 1809 about 60 miles east of Atlanta, Madison has many antebellum homes that remain much as they were in the mid-nineteenth century. By 1840, Madison was known as the most cultured and aristocratic town on the stagecoach route from Charleston to New Orleans. It was spared from General Sherman's burning because U.S. Sen. Joshua Hill, a Madison resident and staunch Unionist, was a friend of Sherman's family and intervened.

CHAMBER OF COMMERCE / **120 Main Street (706-342-4454)** ✦ Madison's home tours, held three times a year, attract visitors from throughout the United States. But during the year most of the houses are private homes and not open to the public. Here are some Madison homes worth seeing: **Foster-Boswell House / Academy Street** ✦ Built around a two-room cabin in 1818, this is an example of how antebellum houses evolved through many additions and updatings. It is now Victorian in style with gingerbread porches. **Carter-Newton House / Academy Street** ✦ Built in 1849 on the site of the burned Madison Male Academy, this two-story Greek Revival is furnished with family heirlooms and antiques.
**Hours**: The Madison-Morgan Cultural Center is

open 10:00 a.m.–4:30 p.m. Monday–Friday and 2:00 p.m.–5:00 p.m. Saturday and Sunday.

**Admission**: A cassette tape and player for walking tours are available for $5.

**Directions**: Take I-20 east from Atlanta to the second Madison exit (Highway 441). Turn right at the first stop light in town, staying on Highway 441. At the four-way stop, turn left. The Chamber of Commerce is on Main Street.

*The Carter-Newton House in Madison survived the Civil War.*

**JONES-TURNELL-MANLEY HOUSE / Main Street (706-342-9627)** ✦ Tours are available of the Jones-Turnell-Manley House, built in 1833, and now home of the Madison Historical Society Headquarters.

**Hours**: 1:30 p.m.–4:30 p.m. Saturdays and Sundays from March 15 to November 15.

**Directions**: Take the second Madison exit (Highway 441). Turn right at the first stop light in town, staying on Highway 441. At the four-way stop, turn left. The Jones-Turnell-Manley House is on Main Street.

# You'll Never Go Hungry Again

## *Where Scarlett Would Eat Today*

Southerners are particularly fond of that scene in *Gone With the Wind* after the war where Scarlett is digging around in the garden at Twelve Oaks and all she can find is one stringy radish. As she raises her fist to the sky and shouts, "As God is my witness, I'm never going to be hungry again," millions of fans make the same vow. Southerners do love to eat, and they love to feed any and all who visit.

A lot has changed in the South since Margaret Mitchell was pounding on her typewriter, but one thing that hasn't changed is Southern hospitality. You'll get it in heaping servings at almost any restaurant you try. And you'll get a few surprises, too. A whole generation of creative chefs has fine-tuned traditional Southern food to make it even better. Call it New South cuisine, if you will, but some of the dishes are downright ingenious. Mammy and Pork never would have thought of Low Country shrimp paste on stone-ground grits or smoked mountain trout on corn cakes.

But if you still have a hankering for more familiar dishes like fried chicken, collard greens, or barbecue, there are plenty of restaurants that serve those, too. In fact, it's probably a good thing Scarlett isn't around today. A few weeks of dining in Atlanta restaurants and she could kiss her 17-inch waist good-bye.

**ANTHONY'S / 3109 Piedmont Road (262-7379)** ✦ This restored 1797 plantation house in Buckhead is a popular tourist attraction, primarily for its antebellum atmosphere.
**Atmosphere:** Old South.
**Cuisine:** American Continental.
**Hours:** 6:00 p.m.–10:00 p.m. Monday–Saturday.
**Prices:** Expensive.
**Dress:** Dressy.
**Reservations:** Yes.
**Payment:** Major credit cards.

**THE BLACK-EYED PEA / 1901 Peachtree Road and other locations around Atlanta (351-5580)** ✦ This restaurant is part of a chain, which means the food is inexpensively priced and consistent in quality. Create your own vegetable plate from black-eyed peas (of course), squash casserole, red beans and rice, fried corn on the cob, mashed potatoes with skins, turnip greens, or a variety of other side dishes. Entrées include meat loaf, country fried steak or chicken, pot roast, turkey, and fish. Yeast rolls and corn bread are delicious. If you have a large family, or you're committed to feeding your in-laws, this is the place where you can fill them up without emptying your wallet.

**Atmosphere:** Wooden tables, country decor.

**Hours:** 11:00 a.m.–10:00 p.m. Sunday–Thursday; 11:00 a.m.–11:00 p.m. Friday and Saturday.

**Prices:** $5 or so for meat and two vegetables.

**Dress:** Casual.

**Reservations:** No.

**Payment:** Major credit cards.

**BOBBY'S AND JUNE'S COUNTRY KITCHEN / 375 14th Street, N.W. (876-3872)** ✦ Sit a spell in the rocking chairs on the porch before going inside, or sit a spell after you sample the fried okra, fried chicken, greens, squash, and other Southern delectables on the menu.

**Atmosphere:** Country; lots of farm implements.

**Hours:** 6:00 a.m.–8:00 p.m. Monday–Friday; 6:00 a.m.–2 p.m Saturday.

**Prices:** Less than $10.

**Dress:** Casual.

**Reservations:** No.

**Payment:** Cash; no credit cards.

┿═ ✦ ═┿

**BURTON'S GRILL / 1029 Edgewood Avenue, N.E. (658-9452)** ✦ This is where Mammy and Rhett would have eaten. Wood and Formica tables are pushed tightly together in a store-front cafe across from the Inman Park MARTA station to accommodate overflow luncheon crowds that include everyone from silk-stockinged lawyers to tattooed rock stars. Owner Deacon Burton died a year or so ago, but his successors have carried on admirably with soul food ranging from fried chicken and collards to fried perch and hoe cakes with black-eyed peas, mashed potatoes, and gravy. Forget your cholesterol count when you come in here, but don't forget desserts like the homemade pound cake and peach cobbler.

**Atmosphere:** Open kitchen, cafeteria-style. Friendly cooks but you have to get your own refills.

*Cook James Hicks serves up more chicken at Burton's Grill.*

Hours: 7:00 a.m.–4:00 p.m. Monday–Friday.
Prices: A bargain at $3.50 or so for a meat and three vegetables.
Dress: Come as you are, but "no shoes, no shirt, no service."
Reservations: No.
Payment: Cash; no credit cards.
Note: No alcohol served.

**Colonnade / 1879 Cheshire Bridge Road, N.E. (874-5462)** ✦ Locals call this the restaurant that time forgot, and there's a definite nostalgic atmosphere about this popular eating establishment. There's nothing outdated about the food, however. Menu items include an assortment of vegetables and entrées from fried catfish and fried scallops to lamb shanks and salmon croquettes. The yeast rolls and corn muffins are highly recommended.
Atmosphere: Diverse clientele dining on wood-grain Formica tables. A separate bar with a fireplace and sofas adds a homey touch.
Hours: 5:00 p.m.–9:00 p.m. Monday–Wednesday; 5:00 p.m.–10:00 p.m. Thursday–Saturday; 11:00 a.m.–9:00 p.m. Sunday; lunch is 11:00 a.m.–2:30 p.m. Monday–Saturday.
Prices: Moderate.
Dress: Casual.
Reservations: No.
Payment: Cash; no credit cards.

*The Horseradish Grill offers a relaxed ambience on the fringes of Chastain Park.*

**HORSERADISH GRILL / 4320 Powers Ferry Road, N.W., across from Chastain Park (255-7277)** ✦ Formerly the Red Barn Inn, the Horseradish Grill is Atlanta's newest purveyor of New South cuisine. Make that Old South cuisine with a New South twist. The Maryland-style fried chicken, for example, is served on hot buttermilk biscuits with tomato gravy, and the cornmeal-crusted catfish is accompanied by cucumbers, greens, and ginger pickled onions with buttermilk dressing.

Other specialties include 21-bean soup, Georgia caviar and crackers (black-eyed peas, sweet pepper relish, and corn crackers), Low Country shrimp paste on grits, Georgia mountain trout wrapped in bacon, or a Southern vegetable sampler plate with choices of turnip greens, Low Country red rice, potato and turnip gratin, whipped sweet potatoes, or thin-crusted jumbo onion rings.

Grilled fish, chicken, and chops are also available for die-hard Yankees.

**Atmosphere:** Country elegant with horsey accessories and Southwest art. A vegetable-herb-flower garden in back adds a nice touch.

**Hours:** 5:00 p.m.–10:00 p.m. Monday–Thursday; 5:00 p.m.–11:00 p.m. Friday-Saturday; 5:00 p.m.–9:00 p.m. Sunday.

**Prices:** Moderate. Entrées range from $5.95 for a cheeseburger to about $19 for veal and lamb.

**Dress:** Casual but upscale to dressy.

**Reservations:** No. Arrive early or expect a lengthy wait.

**Payment:** Major credit cards.

**KUDZU CAFE /3215 Peachtree Road, N.E. (262-0661)** ✦ Located in fashionable Buckhead—but then all of Buckhead is fashionable—the Kudzu Cafe serves up Southern food with a contemporary flair. Sample the fried green tomatoes if you like, but by all means try the hush puppies and fried onion rings with either the grilled grouper with corn relish or the jalapeño-laced crab cakes. For hard-to-fill-up diners, the grilled pork chop, mashed red potatoes (with skins), and sautéed spinach followed by either the frozen Moon Pie or peach cobbler should do the trick. Those who leave without sampling the pecan pie with whipped cream will never forgive themselves.

**Atmosphere:** Yuppie comfortable.

**Hours:** 11:00 a.m.–11:00 p.m. Sundays–Thursdays; 11:00 a.m.–midnight Fridays–Saturdays.

**Prices:** From about $10 to $16 for entrées.

**Dress:** Casual to dressy.

**Reservations:** No.

**Payment:** Major credit cards.

**LICKSKILLET FARM RESTAURANT / 1380 Old Roswell Road, Roswell (475-6484)** ✦ Here is where Scarlett would have sent her carpetbagger visitors. The 1846 farmhouse was the home of Arthur Camp, who dammed the stream called Four Killer Creek and built a flour mill before the Civil War. The road that passes in front of the restaurant was the main road running north out of Roswell to Cumming and was heavily used by Union and Confederate armies. The house was used for a brief time as a Yankee hospital.

Opened as an eating establishment in 1961, Lickskillet Farm Restaurant is strong on country atmosphere and a little short on Southern cooking. Friendly waiters will bring out a pone of cracklin' corn bread served in an individual cast-iron skillet, and diners can sample the Everglades frog legs or the venison tenderloin tournedos with marsala sauce, but you won't find nary a black-eyed pea or turnip green on the menu. A Sunday champagne brunch at least offers country ham and redeye gravy.

The quiet, woodsy setting can't be beat, however, for a romantic evening. Grab a glass of wine and stroll around the landscaped grounds down to Foe Killer Creek (the name was changed for either historic or semantic reasons in the late nineteenth century), or wander over to the Williamsburg-style kitchen garden where fresh herbs, peppers, and vegetables are grown for use in the kitchen.

**Atmosphere:** White tablecloths, soft lighting in a country farmhouse.

**Hours:** Open for lunch Tuesday–Friday 11:30 a.m.–2:00 p.m.; dinner Tuesday–Saturday 6:00 p.m.–10:00 p.m.; Sunday 11:00 a.m.–2:00 p.m.; dinner 5:30 p.m.–9:00 p.m.

**Prices:** From $9.95 to $19.95 for dinner entrées; Sunday brunch is $16.95 for adults, $8.95 for children 6–10, and $4.95 for children 3–5.

**Dress:** Casual to Sunday best.

**Reservations:** No.

**Payment:** Major credit cards.

**MAGNOLIA TEA ROOM / 5459 E. Mountain Street Stone Mountain (498-6304) ✦** There's ambience to spare in this restaurant located in a white antebellum house. Chicken, Southern dishes, and biscuits are specialties, but visiting Yankees in the crowd have a choice of prime rib and fish.

**Atmosphere:** Old South.

**Hours:** Monday–Saturday 8:00 a.m.–2:00 p.m.; Sunday noon–7:00 p.m.

**Prices:** From $10 to $15 for entrées.

**Dress:** Casual.

**Reservations:** Yes.

**Payment:** Cash; no credit cards.

**THE MANSION / 179 Ponce de Leon Avenue (876-0727)** ✦ An elegant, Old South atmosphere is the selling point of the Mansion, which is on the National Register of Historic Places. Southern food such as Georgia trout and sweet potatoes in currant sauce is offered, but locals usually relax over a drink, enjoy the ambience, and eat elsewhere.

**Atmosphere:** Lots of it, with polished dark paneling and Southern touches.

**Hours:** 11:00 a.m.–2:00 p.m. Monday–Saturday; 6:00 p.m.–9:00 p.m. Monday–Sunday; 11:00 a.m.–2:30 p.m. Sunday brunch.

**Prices:** Moderate to expensive.

**Reservations:** Yes.

**Payment:** Major credit cards.

*Mary Mac's is a long-time favorite of Atlanta residents.*

**MARY MAC'S TEA ROOM / 224 Ponce de Leon Avenue (876-6604)** ✦ Just down the street from the Road to Tara Museum at the Georgian Terrace, Mary Mac's is an Atlanta institution and a favorite of locals. It's known for good, plain Southern meats and vegetables in generous quantities. Diners are given pencils to write their own orders from a menu crowded with selections ranging from baked chicken to fried salmon patties, from creamed corn to collard greens. Adventuresome Yankees are urged to try the pot liquor and corn bread. No, pot liquor is not some new street drug; it's the delicious broth that's left when you cook greens. While you'll be tempted to fill up on the fresh vegetables, be sure to leave enough room for the boiled custard or other homemade desserts.

**Atmosphere:** Down-home casual with lots of Formica. A good place for people watching.

**Hours:** 11:00 a.m.–4:00 p.m. and 5:00 p.m.–8:00 p.m. Monday–Friday.

**Prices:** From about $5 and up, depending on the entrée and number of vegetables.

**Dress:** Casual.

**Reservations:** No.

**Payment:** Cash; no credit cards.

**PASCHAL'S RESTAURANT / 830 Martin Luther King Jr. Drive (577-3150)** ✦ Scarlett would not have dared venture to Paschal's, but this is where you'll find students, politicians, businessmen, and the elite of Atlanta's black community dining on some of the best soul food in town. The Atlanta institution was a favorite hangout for Ralph Abernathy, Martin Luther King, Jr., and Andrew Young during the civil rights movement. White liberals and politicians seeking black support also have been known to partake of the excellent fried chicken, barbecue, corn muffins, and peach cobbler. Early birds can stop by for a Southern breakfast guaranteed to rectify cholesterol levels that are too low.

**Hours:** 7:30 a.m.–11:00 p.m. Monday–Saturday. 8:30 a.m.–11:00 p.m. Sunday.

**Prices**: Inexpensive.
**Dress**: Casual or businesswear.
**Reservations**: Yes.
**Payment**: Major credit cards.

**PITTYPAT'S PORCH / 25 International Boulevard (525-8228)** ✦ A favorite spot for tourists, this downtown restaurant is better known for its antebellum atmosphere than its food. Named for Aunt Pittypat Hamilton, the restaurant features an upstairs porch where guests can sit in rocking chairs and sip mint juleps or stroll around and look at the array of photographs, letters, and sketches from the book and movie.

As the story goes, whenever Scarlett visited her aunt in Atlanta, Pittypat would always fix her favorite recipes. The tradition of Southern hospitality continues with entrées such as pork tenderloin with apple and sweet potato purée, Savannah crab cakes, coastal venison pie in a souvenir skillet, and Twelve Oaks barbecue ribs. Desserts include black bottom pie, Bourbon Street bread pudding, pecan pie, or old-fashioned peach cobbler.

Open since 1967, Pittypat's recently has been restored and updated under new owners.
**Atmosphere**: Antebellum style.
**Hours**: 5:00 p.m.–9:00 p.m. Sunday–Thursday; 5:00 p.m.–10:00 p.m. Friday and Saturday. Breakfast and lunches can be arranged in advance for groups of 30 or more.

*Pittypat's Porch serves a bounty of Southern foods.*

**Prices:** Around $20 for entrées.
**Dress:** Casual.
**Reservations:** No.
**Payment:** Major credit cards.

**SOUTH CITY KITCHEN / 1144 Crescent Avenue,
N.W. (873-7358)** ✦ Rhett probably would take one

look at the menu of this trendy Midtown restaurant
and exclaim, "Look what they've done to my grits!"
The she-crab soup would still be familiar to the
Charleston swashbuckler, but everything else has a
definite New South taste. There are dishes for carpet-
baggers ranging from salmon quesadilla to seafood
sausage, but locals would recommend the shrimp and
scallops served over grits, the poached eggs served
over country ham and grits cake, or the grilled quail.
All eaten with biscuits or corn muffins, of course.

**Atmosphere:** A clean, well-lighted place with a white
decor and lots of glass in a converted bungalow.

*South City Kitchen adds a modern touch to traditional dishes.*

Hours: 11:00 a.m.–11:00 p.m. Monday–Thursday; 11:00 a.m.–midnight Friday and Saturday; 11:00 a.m.–11:00 p.m. Sunday.
Prices: Moderate.
Dress: Upscale casual.
Reservations: No.
Payment: Major credit cards.
Note: No wheelchair access.

THELMA'S KITCHEN / 190 Luckie Street, N.W. (688-5855) ✦ A favorite of the downtown lunch crowd, Thelma's serves plain and plentiful Southern soul food. Choose from fried chicken and daily specials accompanied by greens, black-eyed peas, okra cakes, yams, or other vegetables. Leave room for the sweet potato pie.
Atmosphere: Soul-food cafeteria.
Hours: 7:30 a.m.–4:30 p.m. Monday–Friday.
Prices: Inexpensive.
Dress: Casual.
Reservations: No.
Payment: Cash; no credit cards.

TRACKSIDE GRILLE / Kennesaw House, just off Park Square, Depot Street, Marietta (427-7770) ✦ Entrées range from salads to chicken, ribs, and beef.

This is a convenient place to eat if you're touring the historic sites around Kennesaw and Marietta.

**Hours:** 11:30 a.m.–9:00 p.m. Monday–Saturday; noon–8:00 p.m. Sunday.

**Prices:** Entrées from $7.95 to $19.95.

**Reservations:** No.

**Payment:** Major credit cards.

**WHISTLE STOP CAFE / Juliette (912-994-3670)** ✦

The fictional restaurant made famous in Fannie Flagg's novel *Fried Green Tomatoes at the Whistle Stop Cafe* and the subsequent film is now an honest-to-goodness eating place. Dine on fried green tomatoes for $2.25 along with home-cooked vegetables and daily specials. To get there, take I-75 south from Atlanta to exit 61; go left on Juliette Road for nine miles. What there is of downtown is found by taking the first right after the stop sign at U.S. 23 and Georgia 87.

**Atmosphere:** Down home, small town.

**Hours:** 8:00 a.m.–2:00 p.m. Monday–Saturday; noon–7:00 p.m. Sunday.

**Prices:** Inexpensive.

**Dress:** Casual.

**Reservations:** No.

**Payment:** Cash; no credit cards.

**1848 HOUSE / 780 South Cobb Drive, Marietta (428-1848)** ✦ Old South meets New South in the classic Greek Revival mansion built in 1848 by Charleston planter and Marietta's first mayor, John Heyward Glover. The house was in the thick of fighting during the Civil War. Now a restaurant and conference center in the middle of 13-acre Bushy Park Plantation, the 1848 House offers appetizers such as cheese grits and shrimp, Charleston she-crab soup, and fried crab cakes and entrées ranging from smoked trout to grilled quail. For dessert, the sweet potato pecan pie with vanilla ice cream comes highly recommended.

Special menus are available for events such as plantation breakfasts and brunches and picnics, and there is space enough to accommodate about 100 guests for receptions.

And there's more. A shuffleboard court has been added, joining other yard games such as badminton, horseshoes, and croquet. Or one of the swings is always available if you care simply to sit and gaze at the herb garden and the cotton patch.

**Atmosphere:** Elegant Old South.
**Hours:** 6:00 p.m.–9:30 p.m. Tuesday–Saturday; 10:30 a.m.–2:30 p.m. Sunday brunch; 5:00 p.m.–8:00 p.m. Sunday dinner.
**Prices:** Less than $10.
**Dress:** Casual to dressy.
**Reservations:** Yes.
**Payment:** Major credit cards.

# Barbecue

Barbecues were important social events in Scarlett's time. In fact, a barbecue is where Scarlett meets Rhett for the first time in one of the early scenes of *Gone With the Wind*. Atlanta has its share of rib shacks, cafes, and restaurants where the practice of cooking pigs over a smoky pit has been raised to an art form. Here are a few worth trying:

**AUBURN AVENUE RIB SHACK / 302 Auburn Avenue, N.E. (523-8315)** ✦ Get a rib dinner for about $7 and try the collards and corn muffins while you're at it.

**DUSTY'S / 1815 Briarcliff Road, N.E. (320-6264)** ✦ North Carolina-style barbecue with delicious hush puppies, all for about $12.

**FAT MATT'S RIB SHACK / 1811 Piedmont Avenue, N.E. (607-1622)** ✦ Sweet-smoked ribs and sweet-sounding jazz for about $14.

**LOWCOUNTRY BARBECUE / 14 Park Place South (522-1546)** ✦ While this barbecue joint primarily is a caterer, you can grab a seat at the counter and get a tasty sandwich for $2.95 or a plate with pork, Brunswick stew, and slaw for about $6.

*Waiter Michael Williams (left) with owner Donald Sprayberry, Sr.*
*The barbecue restaurant in Newnan was a favorite stop for the late*
*Lewis Grizzard.*

**SPRAYBERRY'S / U.S. 29, Newnan (404-253-4421)** ✦ This was a favorite hangout of Atlanta's other famous writer, the late newspaper columnist and author Lewis Grizzard. Ask for the outside sliced pork sandwich and Brunswick stew for around $5.

**SPICED RIGHT BARBECUE / 5364 Highway 29, Lilburn (564-0355)** ✦ Consistent winners in barbecue cook-offs. Order off the menu or belly up to the buffet for cole slaw, Brunswick stew, beans, potato salad, corn bread, barbecue pork, chicken, and beef. Monday night is all-you-can-eat ribs night for about $11.

# SCARLETT FOR SALE

## Stores That Deal in GWTW Collectibles

UNDERGROUND ATLANTA / **Peachtree and Alabama streets (523-2311)** This new section of stores, restaurants, night clubs, and carts was the street level of the city before the 1920s. A Zero Mile Marker in the midst of the shops bears the inscription "W&A RR," which refers to the Western and Atlantic Railroad and marks the starting point of the railroad back when Atlanta was known as Terminus. Atlanta spread outward from the zero milepost to become a rail hub of the region with four intersecting lines at the time of the Civil War. One block east of Underground is the Freight Depot, built after the Civil War to replace a similar structure burned by Sherman's troops in 1864. The freight depot is shown in several scenes in *GWTW*. The famous open-air hospital scene with hundreds of wounded and dying soldiers lying in the street took place next to the depot.

While in Underground, stop by the **Tara Cart** and let a friend take your picture in a Scarlett O'Hara cutout. Or look over the cart's selection of *GWTW* magnets, games, curios, T-shirts, and Scarlett dolls.

**The Georgia Grande General Store** also sells *GWTW* merchandise, along with a special *GWTW* souvenir edition of the 1939 *Atlanta Journal*, which covered all the activities surrounding the gala premiere of the movie.

**Antiquities** in Underground has more expensive *GWTW* souvenirs, including signed photographs from some of the actors and actresses in the movie. This store offers autographs, letters, first editions, and signed photos of Margaret Mitchell as well as the other stars of *GWTW*. The Underground Atlanta location specializes in the Mitchell and *GWTW* items. One nicely framed photograph of Clark Gable with his autograph and a scene from the movie can be yours for $1,950. Other less costly autographs are frequently available.

For more personal mementos, **Wolf Camera** offers period photographs of customers dressed in costume. Deck you and your significant other out in Civil War outfits for $11.95. Individual photos are $9.95 plus $2 for each additional person.

**Hours:** Underground Atlanta is open 10:00 a.m.–9:30 p.m. Monday–Saturday; noon–6:00 p.m. Sunday.

**Admission:** None.

**Directions:** Underground is two blocks east of the state capitol between Peachtree Street and Central Avenue. Or take MARTA and exit at the Five Points Station onto Peachtree Street and cross over to Underground.

## C. DICKENS FINE RARE AND COLLECTIBLE BOOKS / Lenox Square, 3393 Peachtree Road (231-3825, orders: 800-548-0376) ✦ The staff at C. Dickens say that anything they get connected to *GWTW* sells well. Items such as autographed photos, ticket stubs, matchbooks, perfume bottles, handkerchiefs, postcards, and luggage tags have all sold. C. Dickens also has various *GWTW* editions for sale, as well as other books dealing with Margaret Mitchell or the movie.

**Directions:** Located in Lenox Square Mall in Buckhead. Take MARTA's north rail line and exit at the Lenox station.

## YESTERYEAR BOOK SHOP INC / 3201 Maple Drive, N.E. (237-0163) ✦ *GWTW* first editions, related books and memorabilia.

**Directions:** Proceed north on Peachtree Street from downtown. Maple Drive is the street before the Peachtree Street–Piedmont Road intersection in Buckhead. Go right on Maple; the book shop is on your left.

**Hours:** Monday–Friday 10:00 a.m.–5:30 p.m.; Saturday 11:00 a.m.–4:30 p.m.

**Payment:** Cash or check; no credit cards.

# THE BATTLE
# OF ATLANTA

The Battle of Atlanta was actually a series of battles from June to September 1864 as the Union forces slowly circled Atlanta like a noose and then squeezed it shut. The first clash near Atlanta was at Kennesaw Mountain north of the city. Then came Peachtree Battle, just across the Chattahoochee north of the fortifications. Next was Decatur and the loss of the rail line running east, then Ezra Church, to the west of the city, and finally Jonesboro, the loss of the last remaining rail line to the south. Margaret Mitchell wrote eloquently of these battles, telling of individual soldiers killed or wounded through the struggle. Chapters 18, 19, and 20 in *GWTW* detail these battles and how they affected those left waiting in Atlanta. Chapter 18 mentions wounded rebels from the Battle of Peachtree Creek being nursed by Scarlett, Aunt Pittypat, and Melanie in Aunt Pittypat's house and front yard. The chapter also tells of the dead from Atlanta's battles being hastily buried at Oakland Cemetery. Chapter 21 brings the casualties from Jonesboro and has Scarlett hunting Dr. Meade among the wounded at the train depot to help deliver Melanie's baby. Chapter 23 tells of Scarlett, Melanie, Rhett, Prissy, and the children fleeing the burning Atlanta after the rebel army has evacuated. In Margaret Mitchell's hands, the battle for Atlanta was as much a turning point for Scarlett as it was for the South.

Here is where you can find the battle sites for a closer look at the terrain:

KENNESAW NATIONAL BATTLEFIELD / **Kennesaw Mountain Drive, Kennesaw (427-4686)** ✦ One of the pivotal battles to keep Sherman's men from taking Atlanta was fought here in June 1864. The rebels fortified the heights of Kennesaw Mountain and held off the attacking federals with cannon, rifles, and even rocks. The Union troops eventually went around the mountain, and the rebels were forced to pull back beyond the Chattahoochee River.

Kennesaw Mountain National Battlefield Park is one of the few Civil War sites to escape commercial and residential development because Union veterans from Illinois, Ohio, and Indiana bought 60 acres of it and installed a monument there; other plots were gradually added. The 2,884-acre site later was presented to the National Park Service.

The nearby town of Kennesaw houses the **Big Shanty Museum,** which is the home of The General, the 1855 steam locomotive stolen by Union soldiers in 1862 during the Andrews Raid. The episode was the subject of Disney's movie *The Great Locomotive Chase.* Other Civil War artifacts are displayed in the museum.

Across the railroad tracks are period stores in the restored downtown shopping district. Don't miss Dent Myers' Civil War Surplus ("The Best Little Warhouse in Dixie"), and don't miss meeting the proprietor, "Wildman" Dent, a Civil War reenactor who is either dead serious about his avocation or who just may be the reincarnation of Stonewall Jackson.

**Hours:** The Park Visitors Center is open 8:30 a.m.–5:30 p.m. daily; the Kennesaw Mountain Battlefield is open 8:00 a.m.–5:30 p.m. daily. The Visitors Center offers a small museum, a video on the battle, and a good bookstore of Civil War–related books.

**Directions:** Take I-75 north from Atlanta and take exits 114B or 116. Directional signs will lead you along Old Highway 41 to the Park Visitors Center. To reach the town of Kennesaw, proceed from the park on the Ernest Barrett Parkway (I-75 Exit 116) three miles northeast to the small town. The town's shopping district is directly across the railroad tracks from the Big Shanty Museum.

**CONFEDERATE CEMETERY AND MARIETTA NATIONAL CEMETERY ✦** Marietta has two Civil War cemeteries in the city limits. The Confederate Cemetery has 3,000 soldiers buried there, and the National Cemetery has more than 10,000 Union soldiers interred, as well as those from five subsequent wars.

**Directions:** Take I-75 north from Atlanta 17 miles. Take exit 112 (South Marietta Loop), and go 3.5 miles to downtown. The Visitor's Center is at 4 Depot Street between the railroad tracks and the restored downtown business district. It can provide information and maps for the cemeteries and the restored antebellum homes in the Marietta historical district.

**Roswell ✦** The co-owner of Roswell Mills was living in Bulloch Hall in 1864, flying the French flag over the mill and Bulloch Hall to prevent the Union army from burning both. The flag saved Bulloch Hall; it didn't save Roswell Mills. The mill was destroyed by Federal troops. The Old Bricks, constructed as housing for mill workers in the 1840s, is restored on Sloan Street and serves as meeting space.

After taking Roswell, Union troops began crossing the Chattahoochee River July 5 at several shallow places at Roswell, Sope Creek, Shallow Ford, Power's Ferry, Pace's Ferry, and near today's Northside Drive. This set up the Battle for Peachtree Creek on July 20.

**Directions:** The Old Bricks is off Atlanta Street behind the Historic Roswell Convention and Visitors Bureau (992-4120).

**SITE OF THE BATTLE OF PEACHTREE CREEK** ✦ Today, the battlefield of the Battle of Peachtree Creek is roughly bounded by I-75, Howell Mill, Northside Drive, Collier Road, Peachtree Battle, and the Peachtree Road area known as Brookwood Hills. There are battle markers on Collier Road at Tanyard Creek Park, at Atlanta Memorial Park on Northside Drive, at Peachtree Battle Park on Peachtree Battle, and on the grounds of Piedmont Hospital on Peachtree Street. The area around the WSB-TV station (1601 West Peachtree Street) was the city's outer fortifications. The Battle of Peachtree Creek was fought north of there.

**Directions**: Take Peachtree Street north from Five Points for 4 miles. Turn left at Collier Road, go 1/2 mile to Tanyard Creek Park, and continue 1/2 mile to Northside Drive. Go right on Northside 1 mile to Woodward Way to Peachtree Battle Park on the left.

**SITE OF THE BATTLE OF ATLANTA** ✦ What is called the Battle of Atlanta was actually the fierce fighting between Decatur and Atlanta for the east rail line to Augusta on July 22. These are the episodes depicted in the painting at the Cyclorama. The battlefield covers an area bounded by Memorial Drive, Wilkinson Drive, Glenwood Avenue, Flat Shoals, Moreland, and DeKalb Avenue directly south of the railroad tracks. A section of fighting north of the railroad tracks is further west and takes in Decatur Street, DeKalb Avenue, and Edgewood Avenue to the Downtown Connector. **Directions:** Take I-20 east from downtown. Exit at Glenwood, Memorial, or Moreland exit and start looking for historical markers. Or take Decatur Street east from downtown. Some of the fiercest fighting took place in what is now the parking lot of the Inman Park/Reynoldstown MARTA Station.

**SITE OF THE BATTLE OF EZRA CHURCH ✦** The Battle of Ezra Church occurred when Southern troops engaged Sherman's men at Ezra Church on the west side of Atlanta before they could cut the rail line south to Jonesboro. Union cavalry had also been sent south to Macon and Andersonville to free Union prisoners but were not successful. The battle on July 28 ranged from today's I-20 west to Ashby Street, Bankhead Highway, Anderson Avenue, Ezra Church Drive, and Chappell Road. **Directions:** Take I-20 west to exit 19 (Ashby Street). Continue down Ashby Street to Bankhead Highway to Chappell Road. Proceed down Chappell Road to Ezra Church Drive and you are now in the middle of the battlefield.

SITE OF THE BATTLE OF JONESBORO ✦ The last of the battles for Atlanta, the Battle of Jonesboro was fought August 31 to September 1, 1864. General Sherman was determined to capture the last open rail line out of Atlanta. The stone railroad depot on Main Street in Jonesboro was erected in 1868 to replace the wooden one burned by the Yankees during this battle. Across the railroad tracks from the depot on North McDonough Street at Johnson Street is the Pat Cleburne Cemetery, a Confederate cemetery named in honor of the commander involved in the fiercest fighting in the Battle of Jonesboro as well as in the Battle of Atlanta a month earlier.

Jonesboro also has the Warren House, the 1839 Stately Oaks, and other antebellum houses to visit. Three and a half miles down Highway 19/41 is Lovejoy. The Crawford-Talmadge House dates from 1835, and adjacent to it is the 1830s Fitzgerald House, which belonged to Margaret Mitchell's great-grandfather.

The Jonesboro battlefield is bounded by Jonesboro Road (Highway 54) along the railroad tracks, Highway 138 (North Avenue), the Flint River, Highway 54 (Fayetteville Road), and College Street.
**Directions:** Take I-75 south off I-285. Get off at exit 76, the Highway 41/19 Jonesboro exit. Take Highway 54 to the right, drive 3.5 miles south to Jonesboro paralleling the railroad tracks. Stay on the road as it changes to Main Street, still paralleling the railroad tracks. The downtown historic district has many markers detailing the surge of fighting through the area.

**CARTER PRESIDENTIAL CENTER / 1 Copenhill Avenue, N.E. (420-5100)** ✦ The Jimmy Carter Presidential Library is built on an elevation called Copen Hill that was part of the Battle of Atlanta and is included in the Cyclorama Painting. Legend has it that General Sherman rested in the front yard of the Augustus Hurt house on this site and gazed on a besieged Atlanta from horseback. He happily reported to President Lincoln on September 2, 1864, that "Atlanta is ours and fairly won." There are several historic markers in the Carter Center parking lot referring to the Battle of Atlanta.
**Directions:** Take I-75/85 north to exit 96A (Boulevard/Glen Iris). At the dead end, turn left. Turn right on Cleburne Avenue and then left into the Carter Center parking lot. Walk around the parking lot to the back of the Carter Center for Sherman's view of today's downtown Atlanta skyline.

The Jonesboro battle as well as the earlier three battles for Atlanta were all costly defeats for the South. After Jonesboro, General Hood's beaten army evacuated Atlanta and left it to be occupied by General Sherman and his men. Atlanta was surrendered by Mayor James M. Calhoun September 2, 1864, at what today is the intersection of Northside Drive and Marietta Street.

# BIBLIOGRAPHY

Bartel, Pauline. *The Complete* Gone With the Wind *Sourcebook*. Taylor Publishing Co., 1993.
————. *The Complete* Gone With the Wind *Trivia Book*. Taylor Publishing Co., 1989.
Bridges, Herb, and Terry C. Boodman. Gone With the Wind: *The Definitive Illustrated History of the Book, the Movie and the Legend*. Simon & Schuster, 1989.
Edwards, Anne. *Road to Tara: The Life of Margaret Mitchell*. Ticknor & Fields, 1983.
Farr, Finis. *Margaret Mitchell of Atlanta, Author of* Gone With the Wind. Avon, 1974 (reprint).
"The *Gone With the Wind* Collector's Newsletter." Ed. John Wiley, Jr. Published quarterly. Subscription $12.00 a year, P.O. Box 2072, Dublin, GA 31040.
Harwell, Richard, ed. Gone With the Wind *as Book and Film*. University of South Carolina Press, 1983.
————. *Margaret Mitchell's* Gone With the Wind *Letters, 1936–1949*. Macmillan, 1976.
Kelly, Dennis. *Kennesaw Mountain and the Atlanta Campaign: A Tour Guide*. Kennesaw Mountain Historical Association, 1990.

McCarley, J. Britt. *The Atlanta Campaign: A Civil War Driving Tour of Atlanta's Battlefields*. Cherokee Publishing Co., 1989.

McDonough, James Lee, and James Pickett Jones. *War So Terrible: Sherman and Atlanta*. W. W. Norton & Company, 1987. (See the Epilogue, "Margaret Mitchell Did Give a Damn," concerning her historical accuracy in writing *Gone With The Wind*, especially as it relates to the Battle of Atlanta.)

Miles, Jim. *Fields of Glory: A History and Tour Guide of the Atlanta Campaign*. Rutledge Hill Press, 1989.

Mitchell, Margaret. *Gone With the Wind*. Macmillan, 1936.

Molt, Cynthia Marylee. Gone With the Wind *on Film: A Complete Reference*. McFarland Publishers, 1990.

Peacock, Jane Bonner, ed. *Margaret Mitchell: A Dynamo Going to Waste, Letters to Allen Edee, 1919–1921*. Peachtree Publishers, 1985.

Pyron, Darden A. *Southern Daughter: The Life of Margaret Mitchell*. Oxford University Press, 1991.

———, ed. *Recasting:* Gone With the Wind *in American Culture*. University Presses of Florida, 1983.

Walker, Marianne. *Margaret Mitchell and John Marsh: The Love Story behind* Gone With the Wind. Peachtree Publishers, 1993.

# INDEX

## A

## B